Sandhill Mist

Seasons on a Centennial Farm

Sandhill Mist

Seasons on a Centennial Farm

Elizabeth M. Rosenow

Elizabeth M Rosenow
'Betsy'

To Didge -
with
love always -
from Janie

SandhillMist Press

Published by

Sandhill Mist Press

Grant Township

Free Soil, MI 49411

ISBN-13: 978-1508677536

ISBN-10: 1508677530

For Ken, Aaron, and Chris,

with love.

Acknowledgements

Thanks to Ellen Lightle, Jeanie Mortensen,

and the West Side Gang.

Special thanks to Eric Harvey for helping me find the strength to go on.

Grateful thanks to Ken for his invaluable computer expertise; always my resident guru.

Sandhill Mist

We sit in the sand on the ridge,
sand in our socks.
Sandhill cranes clatter overhead,
three, circling, seeking the marsh.

Last season's bracken is silver on the sand,
this autumn's bronze, some yet gold;
lichens and mosses, green patches,
with sour sorrel on the sterile soil.

Pine cones, silvered by the weather,
lie on the sand for years,
yielding slowly to the sharp silicon,
pretty in their pale way.

We wait for the deer-- they dance
daily with the turkeys.
Entangled tracks prove the pavane,
sand scattered by the polka.

We wait in vain, the deer
pass through at dusk or dawn
or a pre-prandial procession,
their schedules, not ours.

Flickers flash by, present in the pines
with squirrel. Always here,
they punctuate the procession of the deer
with peasant comfort and panache.

Table of Contents

Fall: 69

Winter: 101

Spring:

Worm Moon

Grass Moon

Planting Moon

Oriole

Black and orange used to be the colors of Halloween.
Black cats, orange pumpkins,
black and orange flavored wax panpipes,
black witches, orange candy corn.

But not now.
Not now.

Black and orange are the colors of spring.
Oranges in the birch tree,
cut in half, just so;
watched with eager anticipation
from red maple flowering
to apple bud.

What day? What hour?
What first burst of tentative warmth
from the closer sun?
The anticipation builds.

Then he arrives.
Like a phoenix from the ashes of winter,
Black and orange,

3

the flame of spring,

the oriole comes in a burst of glory.

Black and orange,

licorice and tangerine,

flame and soot.

Spring is here in all its finery.

Winter is vanquished.

Even if bird eagerly sips juice

amidst the wet snowflakes

of aberrant May storm,

Spring is here.

Corvus

Jagged torn slashes of night
whip through the coiling chilling day,
shrieking over the wind.
Carrion, that rotten flesh,
their choice on which to dine.
Screaming, the wind
drives them to ground.
The carrion
makes black plumage,
scraps of gloom.
Doom.

Early Spring

The red-winged blackbirds sing,
crazily clutching last year's reeds
down at the frozen pond.
The ice that grew soft and rotten
in the February thaw
now lies ridged and rigid,
not a glassy reflection;
too ribbed for skates.
Crystal tomb for precocious tadpoles,
polliwogs that fed the early birds
when they came from farther south, perhaps
where winter does not play tricks with spring.

Spring Sabbatical

The swelling spring days beckon
with a crystal call that won't be denied.
Come, come to the waxing woods
before the wakening trees shade out
the wonder below.
White toothwort and trillium,
golden trout lily with dappled blades.
Squirrel corn and Dutchman's breeches
hanging out to dry on the ferny foliage.
Delicate spring beauty blooms-
this pink porcelain treasure.
The wonders of wintergreen
upon which white bells
share the fragrant leathery leaves
with gems of red berries.
Violets, violent in their abundance
bless us with white, purple and yellow
and delicious fragrance and flavor.

This garden, The Garden

Spring, Serious

The skies, crystal blue or leaden,

bare the cruel, fickle face of spring.

Verdant sprouts are extruded from warm brown earth,

to be smothered with white killing frost.

A mantle of shimmering ice may grip the land,

fought back with bits of salt, and sand,

and embattled emissaries of phone and wire,

fire and ambulance.

Winter's blast is never so unkind.

Prepared then are we, with parkas and piles of wood against

the house,

and larders stocked from end to end with food,

rib-sticking, and candles, and extra socks.

Summer's heat is fought with languor.

Her thunderheads resound with relief.

In autumn, we expect the leaves to be torn

from trees with howling winds,

and blasts of sleet to smite the plundered gardens.

But spring is hope,

and hope crushed again.

And again before the warmer winds
wind among the apple blossom hills
and jeweled migrants do not drop from icy clouds,
betrayed by traitor sunbeams in the south.

Reluctant Spring

Spring is tugging at my reluctant heart.

Daffodils, fruit flowers,

sun on my shoulder, warm rain...

How can I still be empty inside

with so much outside my skin?

Breezes blow, birds sing,

I sit like a rock.

Hollow,

empty,

dark.

Susurrations

And we are the future and the past, blurring the present in our motion through it; a hummingbird in the spray of a garden hose; a molting hen with the eggs of tomorrow already in her; a sheep, rooing yesterday's wool over the soft and springy fleece of tomorrow. We are the arcs of meteors, the progress of the zodiac, the circle of the seasons from Persephone to Hades to Demeter.

I eat a winter apple, cidery sweet with the scent of blossom; an omelet, full of sprouting fall onions and today's egg. I bake today's bread with the last of the wheat, and soak bean seeds for tomorrow's sprouts. The fawn that creeps through the morning mist is the buck I will shoot next November. The cat sleeps, twitching with dreams of the mouse she will eat that will become cat.

Last winter's snowmelt still fills the streams. As cirrus clouds give way to towering cumulus, I breathe in summer thunderstorm after spring zephyr. I creep, walk, run, walk, and creep again.

I am.

The Dregs of Night

She stood alone in the dregs of night, twirling the remains of
the stars between her fingers, smooth as talc, the planets
gritty as sand-

The pale expressionless moon watched from behind the
sycamore, her tresses caught up in the branches, a tangled
skein of silk-

Permeating Rain

Permeating rain changes sullenly
into the particularly wet snow of spring.
Sparrows bathe in spreading puddles,
shivering clean, beak to feet.

Seedlings huddle in greenhouse
stunted by lack of sun
yet whiteflies flourish.

Clouds separate for watery light,
late afternoon,
not changing the monochromatic sky.

Lambs huddle under wet ewes
seeking warm milk and shelter
as mothers chew and meditate
on the late season.

Barn swallows are trapped
far to the south by the
wall of weather, inclement,
that still promises mayflies,
mayflowers.

May it yet come.

Hive

chill wet spring morning
bees cluster on the hexagons
humming, humming
unwilling to venture out
for cold early suns of dandelions
caterpillars of willow catkins

dying bees are thrust out
by busy sisters
to pile on the ground, mumbling
to blow away, tumbling
in the oxymoron of a cold zephyr

no nectar, no honey, no pollen
for waxen comb latticed
structured by blind obedience
to a wisp of a brain, to higher power
to vagaries of the weather
this dragging season, this wet spring

Sparrowing

delicate porcelain of spring beauty gyres with the

crackling song sparrow amidst the

turbulence of twisted-stalk, arbutus

toothwort and trillium gladly the song sparrow trills

over the forest of foreign barberry topped

by blighted beeches even the ashes decline

that ubiquitous emerald burrowing beetle as

maples go on and on with

spring leeches of sap for syrup

hemlocks' dark brooding presence looms over

woodferns' delicate green bouquets escaping

to the arms of the froth of

juneberry shadblow now

berries in June unbearable crimson purple come October that

unspeakable month of glory and decay

riot and rot

as must we all

Ewes Relaxing in the Field

Tansy and Sedge, content in the sun
chew their cuds

Rose wanders, free of her
place in the tyranny of barnyards

Hen, Sage and Gerri
peer into the barn for bits of hay

The snow has receded
cranes clatter beneath the clouds

Robins sing-in the spring
Soon, lambs will come to play

in greening pastures
We are content in the sun

as our plans blossom with the crocus
and the season unfolds

The Tiny Spark

The black lamb
in the lime green towel
lay in my arms all night
His breaths
hesitant and halting
kept hope awake
Dried and rubbed
pressed and caressed
I held him
till morning
Finally
the tiny spark fluttered
and went out.

The Cat Watches the Lava Lamp

April sun pierces the window,
sparkling the dust motes.

The cat naps on the braided rug.

Vivaldi eases the noonday,
Dvorak, dinner.

The cat dabs at the aquarium clownfish.

Boiling, baking, cooking, cleaning,
the day consumes itself.

The cat stares at the lava lamp.

Folding sheets in front of the tv,
Nature, Nova, talking heads.

The cat presses a cricket under a paw.

The sun sets, April moon
eclipsing the light of the lava lamp.

The cat sleeps on the foot of the bed, twitching.

The morning fog

rolls and presses on me

like honey

as I walk to the barn

to let the sheep out to pasture

Opening the carabiner

on the chained gate

I see them push through the mist

and disappear

If I follow

would I disappear

emerging somewhere else?

The fog rolls on

thick as eggwhite

Above, there must be dawn

Thus Wooled

Sheep slip into the pasture
Fog gathers on their stocky frames
Thus wooled, they graze
revealed by the creeping sun
transmuting brome and knapweed
into milk and meat

Sun creeps onto still pond
changing dull to hard bright
eclipsing frogs till night
again brings forth their
chiming, bright as the sun did shine

Mist shrouds the hive
entrance with only one bee
peeking, awaiting warmth
and light for flight
to dewy blooms, honey stomachs to fill
damp pollen to pack in baskets

Light awakens the house
of people, dulling the shine with
workaday burdens while frogs sleep
sheep graze, bees eat
all blessed again
by darkness, mist and moonlight

Fog at 8 AM

The air is white wool
as hard to see as it is to breathe
Even sounds are muffled
The hungry sheep
the morning birdsong
the frogs in the little pond
where the cranes nest
where the redwings hang wobbly
from reeds and cattails

My mind is white wool
as hard to see as it is to breathe
Even thoughts are muffled
The sad reaching
the morning plans
The ideas of the new day
encrusted with the old
When thoughts collide
wobbly from yens and yearnings

Sun rises higher in the sky
burning off the mist
clearing the air for a new day

New beginnings

New pasture

Aroma of arabica beans

Distant vistas

Lightening of being

Lightening of beings

Sheep, cranes, redwings, frogs

And me

Labor

The laboring ewe pants,
arches her back,
and finally slips out the lamb
in its sac.
She licks it off.

The lamb struggles
and stands,
seeking,
seeking,
tottering, tottering,
tentatively calling,
kneeling at the milky altar.

Satisfied, it rests,
a little pile
of curly wet wool.

Building Up the Barn

The cloistered basement lay for a hundred years

covered with only a tin roof for fifty

after freak a tornado took the top

leaving only the old stalls of horses

stanchions of forgotten cows

old fossil feather of a chicken long gone

Until after the century

grandson of grandson

built back the top

for fragrant hay laid by

for the sheep below

in the old stalls of horses

and where the stanchions were

where the feather lay

beneath the store of hay

put by each year for

another hundred years

by the grandsons of grandsons hence

Closeted Dreams

The seed potato
already encrusted with tentacles of sprouts
snuggled into the warm earth
nuzzling stones and soil
seeking nourishment from rocks and rain
Leaves finally poked through
seeking the sun through the quilted mulch
the sweet sheep manure
finally to photosynthesize and multiply
in the cool blanket of hay
that keeps the weeds at bay
till in the fall the fork seeks
buried treasure
tasty nuggets to store and savor
Frites and fries, gravy, au gratin
escalloped, creamed, baked and boiled
for salad, with onion (a story all its own)

Closeted dreams
basking in baskets of winter

·

Telescope

In the night we exchange places
with the stars, through a tube.

Will stars know what to do,
amongst the bushes and chickens?

We will know what to do
in the navy blue sky.

We will become constellations.

Summer:

Strawberry Moon

Thunder Moon

Green Corn Moon

The Hay, Mowed Yesterday

I drive the vintage Farmall
pulling the wagon piled high
with sweet bales
The thump-thump of the baler
all afternoon
follows the clack-clatter of the rake
rustling the slender stalks
into windrows in the dried-off dew
The hay, mowed yesterday
(including the stripe of snake)
makes scented sweetness
in the sun

The bales rise high in the barn
thoughtfully stacked
We are weary, sweaty
Bits of sharp
clinging all over

Below in the barn
the sheep wait patiently
The hens announce each egg
The cats sleep on a feed bag

I drive the vintage Farmall
and help stack

When Will We Rest

When bee's asleep in bowels of flower,
powdered with pollen,
bee's eyelashes aflutter
in honey dreams.
When wren seeks her rest
inside the hollow house,
fledglings safely tucked under.

When sheep are bedded in the barn,
lambs along ewes.
The rams alone.
Hens at roost,
quiet at last,
with morning's eggs becoming.
Opossum has crept under eaves
seeking shelter, lazy from the storm.

Barn cats curled, coiled
in deep nests of hay,
oblivious to mice,
mice indeed asleep in corn.
The hay itself at rest.

Linnaea borealis

Twinflower

Slender seeking stems
twinned trumpets
pink, meander the moss
with delicacy
I trace them with my fingers
feeling the embroidery
Looking inside the tiny pink bells
a hand lens reveals delicate fur
This small grace and glory
rises, empowering pines
hemlocks, spruce
with humble beauty
and pervasive grace
Tiny tremblings of hope
nibble away the day's
enduring doom
with the small joys
of peace

Checking the Hay

Running the gauntlet of tall stems on the way
to check the hay
risk of ticks
It lies in the field in layers
still dripping with dew at nine in the morning
It will dry by midday
Raked into windrows in sun by one
Baled at three
In the lofty barn by night

The fulfillment
of a promise to the patience of sheep.

Haying Before the Storm

Till the night, verdant to black,
we lift fragrant bales
onto the wagon
with a hoist from one knee.
That leg of the jeans
will wear out first.

The day is hot.
Crumbs of prickly hay
stick to every inch
of our weary bodies.

Sharp lightning already dances
over the Big Lake.
But we have won the day.
The wagon creaks slowly
up to the dim barn.

Tomorrow the territory
of the barn swallows
will be that much smaller.

The Scent of Hay

We stood looking at the hay-
cut, raked, baled, loaded, unloaded, stacked.
Just looking at the sweet hay
and a little brown bat,
that flickered
and flew away in the twilight.

Grass crisped on the undulating fields.
Swallows swooped for insects
for two toasty days.

Dusk darkened. No moon.
Fireflies glided about.
We couldn't see the hay
but its scent seeped into the night.

Waiting

Solemn violets
Staid old ladies
with dainty perfume
fill my garden.
Creeping from their beds
they greet the day
in the purple
they can finally wear
after the colors
of youth
have been put aside.
Waiting in vain
for visitors:
Hummingbirds, bees,
are elsewhere.

The Ram Lamb

on the twisted steel wire
of the cross-brace on the corner of the pasture fence
hung himself.
Wedged in, his curved horn
sealed his fate.

The other lambs clustered around.
His mother, in the next pasture, called
and called,
as mothers do...

And calls…

Hoggets

The second-summer lambs
getting fatter, growing thicker fleeces
than the ewes nursing newborns,
walk with them down the path to the pasture,
picking up their feet, following the trail
trodden by many hooves to the food,
the pasture of grass, knapweed, alyssum
and butterflies. The cats follow,
tracing patterns between the sheep,
twining against them in mutual friendship.
Thus the procession, the progress
of the season. September brings more
independence. Wethers to keep company
with ram lambs. Ewe lambs with ewes
are weaned by mutual disinterest. The
rams rest and eat, with hard labor to come
for which they wait in anticipation
of a kind of lovemaking that brings the
next season of ewes with lambs, hoggets,
wethers, rams. Thus proceeds the way
interrupted by death, planned or otherwise
as time goes on as it is wont to do.

Heat Wave

The chickens pant in July
still peckish, and peck-ish
They quarrel querulously
at the corn and oats in the pan
They pant in the sun
They pant in the shade
in the inexorable heat
the execrable warmth
Breeze or not
Kitchen scraps from the garden are pecked
picking only the choicest and juiciest
The huge arugula, the cracked tomato
Scorning cucumber peels and radish ends
in petulance
Prima donnas in the barnyard
Queens of the coop
Bitter children in the heat
Longing for the night's cool moon.

Sullenly Seeking Shade

Cornstalks twisted, gaunt and sere,
earthworms crusty, knurled and shrunk.
Drought suckles moisture from tepid lake
which offers no refreshing dip.

Parched pastures, mirage of food
to panting sheep, craving salt.
Chickens scratching grey-brown dust
search vainly crickets, greens and grubs.

Barncats sullenly seeking shade
stretch out on bales of crispy hay.
The still shade of the woodlot rings
with cicadas' drone refrain.

We pause in front of noisy fans,
awaiting fall, its frosty morns,
already regretting summer's gifts
that we could not accept with grace.

Scrap

In the house
a moth clings to fresh-picked laundry
a silken scrap amongst the
cotton sheets and nightgowns.
Carefully cupping my hands, so as
not to damage fragile feathers,
I take it to the open window
where it clings
strangely reluctant,
suddenly loathe to leave.

With the moon to light the way
it releases its grip
and gusts away.

Red Clover

the tightly tiered rosy pink pagodas

whose sweet centers seek

striped bees

the green trefoils, hairy edges

with a pale line tracing

luck is here with

trefoil plus one

four-leaf, lucky

as the foot

of an

unlucky

rabbit

their meadow is shared with

daisies, love me or not

milkweed, mother of monarchs

buttercups of gold

sedges with edges

round rushes

and grasses

voles, cricket frogs, toads

and an

unlucky

rabbit

above fly kestrels and harriers

not above a lunch of vole

or mouse

or frog

or great leaping grasshopper

whose wings flap and glide

or an

unlucky

rabbit

Ova

The hens take turns on the nests.

They trill, and cluck.

The appearance of a warm egg, finally,

is greeted with whoops of delight,

or pride, or pain.

The hen jumps out, exhilarated.

Another sidles in to take her place.

She feels the warm egg pressing against her breast.

She grows dreamy.

This egg she will nurture, or perhaps it will nurture others.

Her breast will comfort a chick, soft downy yellow with

      stripes of chocolate brown.

Or the egg is comfort food for the folks who bring her food,

corn, oats, soy, soft tomatoes, split cabbages, wizened apples

in exchange for fried egg sandwiches with mustard,

scrambled eggs with ham,

hard-boiled eggs, dyed or decorated even in July

to set them apart from eggs uncooked.

Omelets with cheddar cheese, scallions, and rosemary.

Pound cakes and pudding, angel cakes and custards.

The hens have names like Angel, Rosemary, Omeletta,

      Chiffon, Henny Penny, and The Little Red Hen.

Why does a hen not lay?

Hormones, calcium shortage.

The choice not to bring an egg into this troubled world, rife
with the dangers of fox and frypan, kettle and owl, weasel and
Easter bunny.

Each hen knows her place.

The Pecking Order is not always kind, or fair, but neither is
        any form of government.

Perhaps a hen is at the bottom of the Order

because she does not lay,

or she can no longer lay,

because she is constantly harassed

by the other hens, and her own insecurity.

Perhaps she wishes to crow.

They vote, and blackball, backstab, and bribe.

They are as coldly unfeeling as cliques of teenage girls.

Hens enjoy a beautiful day.

Rain drives them under the coop, fretting about a

Bad Feather Day.

Hens appreciate fresh bedding, fresh water, and treats.

They come running from all directions when a person
        approaches.

They run erect with legs outstretched, like ostriches.

A small step for a hen,

But a giant leap for chickenkind.

Dreams

The cratered plate in the sky,
the wide thighs of the night,
the owl, the night heron,
cedar-scented velvet is the summer eve.

Behind the yellow squares of light
the people stand
and stare, looking out,
listening.
But outside the foxes feel the quickening,
quiet and alert.
Night rabbits range
with one ear perked,
knowing the fox,
feeling the fear,
yet clovering nonetheless.

The people are staring at the flickering blue box
dumb to the breeze, to the
bats seeking moths before morning.
They retire, dumb to the deafening silence
as frogs halt their chorus
while whippoorwills soar,

sweeping mosquitoes into their
fringed mouths.

The people dream
of houses and streets
cars and work.

Come dawn, the dreams outside
are of the moon
the bounty of life
and the chase.

Pearl and Soot

Moon-pie split by its diameter,
half snow, half coal,
half glowing in the luminous light of night,
its alter, shade.
It holds its secrets, its silent
footprints, its flags.
Bat flits across dark in the light,
chasing white moth in shadow.
A breeze fitfully lifts, and drops,
setting pale undersides of flat leaves
against the sky.
Constellations of mosquitoes,
heard, not seen,
complicate the sliding-away day.

Waning or waxing, the moon
slips below the horizon.
We sleep unaware
that it may grace another hemisphere.

Bat, moth, mosquito,
flat leaves are still.
Lightning bug winks once more,
winks out.

Stars burn brighter

before fading to pink

as another orb takes the sky.

Slick, a brook trout

slipped through my dangling fingers
in the cold clear stream
as I dipped
into gelid water
on the hot August afternoon.
Green gelatin strands of algae
caressed my hand
from careless rocks
dappling the gleaming sand.
The summer sun
hung languidly
across the forest canopy above.
In between sky and water
warblers stitched song
through the traceries of lady fern.
Dragonflies plied their craft
above the creek.
Frogs plopped
loud as skipped stones
and the flat turtles
slipped silently away
from the mossed log.

Water striders dimpled

their way across the invisible membrane.

The soft zephyr

grew fitful and died.

Mosquitoes emerged from nowhere

sending me somewhere else.

Daisies in the Hay

Leucanthemum vulgare

Staring deep into a daisy
eyes tracking the whorls in the gold glowing disk
a Fibonacci sequence of intersecting arches
Thrips clamber drunkenly over the yellow hills
veering though overlapping vortices
of this lonesome isolated landscape
So alike and so far is each white petaled blossom
as I loom over the bees and blooms
tracing the sequence in each single
flower with its thrips, its bees
gorging in golden gluttony
as are my eyes

Danger

The ewes circle, nuzzling the sleeping lambs, nickering softly.
They will rest only when they are sure all is well.
A mouthful of hay, a sip of water- all secondary to
        watchfulness.
A wolf may come. All they can do is insert themselves
        between lamb and danger.
The lambs grow up.
Danger comes. The tie is still there.
All the ewes can do is watch.

Make Believe

that the sky isn't falling, Chicken Little.
That the fox won't come, or the hawk.
Make believe that the grain will come
and the corn.

Make believe that hummingbirds won't fall from the sky
        in a sudden storm.
That the snake won't swallow the sparrow's egg.
Make believe that the sun will shine
and gentle rain will come
in its time.

Make believe that death won't pour from the sky
or rise up from the ground.
That men will live in peace
in freedom, and joy.

Make believe.

Make believe.

kindergarten round-up

vaccinations, vitamins
short little horns, sharp hooves
of the half-grown halflings
bruised, I hug the wooly honeys as they
roll and tumble
ewes calling, babies bleating baa!
barn in an uproar, suddenly silent
as families reunite, lambs quiet now
quickly grabbing a gulp of rich milk
hay settles down, ewes cluster for apple treats
order restored
mission accomplished

lambs, lambs across the world
so many will be sacrificed
at the altars of hunger and love
why

The First Pullet Egg

appeared today, a curiosity
in the chicken yard

This first was a surprise
No maternal feelings here
No snuggling against downy breast

It rolled among tattered stalks
of tansy, brome, and goldenrod
fertile as a thought
that passes alone along the day

Crimson Tide

The chickens are killing each other
Bloodthirsty beaks find the soft tissue
of hens weak from producing an egg
Leghorns' white plumes are etched in crimson
as they dance in proud frenzy
Exultant, desperate, carelessly cruel
Hungry for a new victim
They chase around and around
harrying each other
The faltering one goes down
A red feather triggers fountains of gore
as wild-eyed the dance goes on and on
One by one
Frittata
Omelet

A single fried egg

It's About Thyme

Herbs line the patio
Green sentinels
of stately rosemary
spires of thyme
or blades of chives
Purple-peaked lavender.

They flank the door
in pots of protection
from prying eyes
from bugs
from savorless suppers.

Herbs even overcome
smoke of grill
scented charcoal
seasoning burger and kebabs
delighting nose and palate.

Honeybees buzz the blossoms
too busy to sting
sweet nectar lips
pollen sacs packed
herb seeds to come.

Herbes de Provence

fines herbes

Shakespeare's herbs

cloistered gardens

and my porch.

Chrysalis

How does one become a butterfly? You must want to fly so much that

you are willing to give up being a caterpillar.

-Trina Paulus

Caterpillar crawls contemplatively

passing places she knew.

Bright banners now tattered, wan, waste.

Appetite gone, gnawing hunger abated, sated.

Honeyed blooms she ignored in the sun

blown, blasted to green seed.

Nodding gold, she slows,

pauses,

ascends ruined stem,

a perch, a dangle.

Slowly a chrysalis appears.

The caterpillar is gone.

Cells, cytoplasm, rearrange.

A long, restless sleep.

The palest green and metallic gold house

splits, and lo,

not a caterpillar appears, with

fleshy body, prolegs, spiracles,
but a crumpled new life form.

Slowly as sunrise
furled wings appear, extend.
New life pulses through black body.
Six shiny legs, sails.
Vivid as an oriole,
she ascends
in all her glory.
Butterfly!

We crawl along on our prolegs
writhing amongst the milkweed leaves.
Chewing, content to plod
and pace our days to sap and sun.

Walking Down to Check the Pears

It's August, it's warm, the Japanese beetles swarm.

It's time to check the pears.

The walk isn't long, and there is

hay to toss to the sheep,

ground squirrel holes to stomp.

(They trip the sheep.)

Knapweed to look at for bees,

honey-, bumble-, both.

Bobolinks, meadowlarks swell the sky with song.

Grasshoppers jump and spit,

startling in their suddenness.

The pears grow and swell.

But not yet ripe, they wait on the stem

for September sun to bring out the sweetness.

We will come back to check again,

past the hay, sheep, squirrel holes, bees both, birds

and

grass

hoppers.

Tussock Moth and Monarch

for Soli and Ceci

Tussock Moth

Caterpillars, black, white, orange, bristled like
bottlebrush from end to end, creep in the company
of fellow travelers across the solemn milkweed
imbibing the poison that saves them, cutting
the vein, the midrib, pressure-releasing the extra
toxin, that mad milk, and stripping the blade bald.
Dusty rose milkweed, bright orange butterflyweed
reduced to sad slender sticks by the incessantly
moving mouthparts, hunger driving them.
They pupate in silent anonymity, emerging not
in glory but unexcelled in drabness, garbed in
plain Quaker gray, no rickrack, no spots, no stripes,
flying at twilight, blindly seeking the artificial light.
Why then do they fly at night? They click inaudibly
to warn bats of foul flavor of the sap they drank.
They seek bitter weed upon which to lay the eggs
that bring in their turn the procession of moving
mouthparts of the bottlebrushes' progress.

Monarch

Milkweed she seeks, a succulent green place
to put out her little barrel-shaped eggs. The
caterpillars come, fleshy green with small stripes
of white, black and yellow, caterpillars, larvae of
light and sunshine. The pupa cases glisten green
gilded with spots of purest gold.
After silence they stir, split and deliver
precious black crumples, not drably but gloriously
pumping in the sun, not Quaker but opulent oriole
unfurling their flags, stretching and seeking
foreign fields, the long Mexican journey.

Hummingbird on Tomato Cage

Fat bumblebee, toy birdie,

tipping tiny head, wings akimbo

Garden jewel, tiny toes

Christmas ornament in August

Does busy mind rest

Does busy buzz subside

Do thoughts dart like dragonflies

or flutter like easy butterflies

Ruby glow in the sunlight

Emerald gleam at the sugarfeeder

To crimson-tubed flowers, to rainbow spray

of garden sprinkler it goes

with tiny toes

Garden jewel.

Bumblebees Tumble

bumblebees tumble, seeking humble homes in hollow ground, bumbling, buzzing to fill cheeks with nectar, pack pollen baskets orange, up before honeybees to plunder, licking the lilac, plunging into the scented blooms, abandoning caution because of strong stings, not humble at all.

honeybees rise, flying in late morning after humming on the threshold, planning, buzzing about the day to come, dancing, prancing in their honey-colored fur, stinging nonetheless, clambering over clover, storing the sweetness of spring.

lambs leap in the lane, grazing the gates as they dash to the pasture, spronking up all feet in the air at once, ewes following sedately except for the occasional self-conscious leap, seeking alfalfa, brome, clover and dandelion, tasting all, rejecting little, filling udders for lambs to eagerly empty.

hens are busy as bees, tasting every plant, fussy as old ladies, cheerful as children as they bathe spread-eagle in the dust, their feet pedaling the dirt as they lose their dignity in the rolling and tumbling, quietly sneaking to the nest to gift us with oblong eggs, brown, blue, green and white.

garden burgeons, squirting shoots to the sun, tendrils, leaflets, strong stems, sweet petals of azure feathery flax, snowy clouds of phlox, pink dewy decked dahlias, and vegetables taking their turn on wormy humus.

april, a torrent to may, tearing into june, slipping into july, panting into august and beyond.

bumblebees relax, honeybees' hexes brim with sweetness, lambs grow up, ewes dry up in turn, flowers ebb and flow as they make seed, vegetables fill pantry and cellar.

The Granite Moth

The granite moth
hits the window screen
slides to the porch floor
wings fluttering heavily
feathery bits of mica
flaking off.
The basalt butterfly
flaps by
with all the insouciance of stone.
The iron ant, the delicate dolomite dragonfly,
the jade mantis.
All clumsy in their stone.
All beautiful in the obsidian night,
the silver coin of the moon.

Thoughts pile heedlessly onto the windowsill,
hit the lamps, again and again,
rise into the dusk
toward the moon
seeking lightness and light...

Labor Day

The sun glares sternly upon the earth.

Scorching heat sends us indoors.

It drives panting sheep off the pasture to shade of the old
        barn.

It evaporates clouds.

Even weeds wither and crisp.

Rhode Island Reds poach gently.

Roses shatter.

Daisy petals count out-

He loves me

Not.

He loves me.

Fall:

Harvest Moon

Hunter's Moon

Frost Moon

Merry Monarchs

Merry monarchs make sweet meals on goldenrod,

earth colors of early fall.

Caterpillar, two black filaments on either end,

striped merrily, greedy green,

munching, munching mouthparts

scallop and scoop milkweed leaf till

only vein remains.

By now, milkweed flowers have podded,

pollinated by persistent long-legged monarchs.

Pods hiding crumpled silken treasure

dry and split, spilling fluff delicate

as dragonflies, each one carrying seed of

next year's

milkweeds,

monarchs,

merry caterpillars.

Picking Dewberries

There's a clearing in the woods,

where the deer walk,

and timberdoodles explode into the sky,

that was a marsh

before the drought years.

Now prickly stems sprawl

over the crisp sphagnum.

Gleaming wine-purple nuggets

wait patiently for my basket.

Dewberries.

Jewels free for the gathering.

Fingers stained purple, torn jeans.

Thorny stigmata.

Free?

The sun presses my shoulders.

If there's a late mosquito,

she will find me.

A bluejay calls.

A dozen chickadees answer.

The robin doesn't look at home here

now that the sun has turned back.

The cranes clatter overhead.

The basket fills slowly.

No telephone here.

I could just stretch out,

sprawl in the crisp sphagnum

and burst those garnet jewels on my tongue.

But then there would be no pie.

Not everyone can turn out a decent pie today.

Not everyone has tasted fresh dewberry pie,

and those who have won't tell.

I share a truth with the Little Red Hen.

Maybe it's just easier to pick the berries alone,

make the pie alone,

and share it anyway.

And she did.

This could be the very center

of the Wilderness.

There are too many berries for the deer to eat.

A slug ate one,

but that's all.

Two hours and a half

crouched above the briers.

Funny that I should feel

Better.

Back-of-the-Farm Tea

To the far forty we go,
past the abandoned house and barn
to the old farm that
this farm engulfed.
Into the woods, the marsh, the meadow
to collect ingredients for a special tea.
A tasty tisane.

Wintergreen, its leathery leaf and
fragrant scarlet berry.
Leaves of sassafras:
the mitten, the blade, the trefoil,
sweet as root beer.
Blueberry bush the deer didn't eat.
Prickly dewberry, leaves and dried fruit.
Handful of the five-bunched needles
of white pine-
just the right amount of resin.

This aromatic beverage
brings the outdoors in
all winter long, and into spring.

Harvest List

Great ruby globes fill the pail.
Hearty, thin-skinned tomatoes
put by for the coming year.
Boiling water, dip, slip the skins
and simmer for hours for sauce.

And chickens, in turn
bright, full of a life to give.
Put by for winter, frozen.
Caught crowing.
Boiling water to slip the feathers.
Quenched in cool.
Drawn, with yellow-jackets
too drunk with blood tasting
to sting. And ducks
fat with quack, meet their fate.

Kale stands strong in rows
till last frost snaps
for soup and a salad.
Crispy greens for health.
Carrots wait in ground till
frost sweetens and they join the soup,
the salad, with earthy flash.
Pears swell and fall to ground

as they sweeten. Beat the deer

and wasps again. Jars fill

with white nectary slices.

Dewberries too- beat the deer

and bears! for garnet

nuggets. Fill pail and jam jar

for winter biscuits.

Dill stings the nose and packs into pickles.

The kitchen aromas roar.

Robins sing for rain,

autumn's balm, dreaming

already of sun and warmth.

Chickadees quicken

dancing hearts, ready for

dancing flakes.

Bluejays caw, and caw again

with sarcasm, also in time

for fall's fallen rainbow.

Squirrels pack the woods with

winter's snack of nuts and cones

as we pack our pantries.

Hope and satisfaction swell

as summer's bounty

punctuates the year

with pleasure and regret.

Preserve September

Save summer in a jar.
Preserve September,
the incandescent days,
the frosty nights,
crisp as a pippin.

Put applesauce in glass.
Dewberries from dewy bramble,
promise of biscuits in December.
Green elephantine heads of cabbage,
golden sauerkraut in crocks
for reubens in January.
Tomatoes, releasing summer promise-
paste and sauce,
pizza in February.

Regarding "Unharvested," Robert Frost's apple fall

The ink flows from his pen like cider,
hard or soft. Apples, hard or soft,
litter the ground under the trees.
Soft, stung with hungry wasps, probing,
probing, always ready to sting.

Hard, growing soft, if not eaten
by apple fawns seeking sweet meal
before does leave safety of the forest.
Smaller bites show from squirrels, from voles,

perhaps rabbits not stung by foxes.
We are greedy to gather apples, drops yet uneaten,
or stretched on tiptoes from boughs that break
under our touch. Pies, betty, jelly, cakes and bread,

waldorf, or just crisped down greedily out of hand.
We are greedy now, as before the fall.
Spring scents the fruit, summer plumps,
autumn reds and juices them, attracting

hordes of hungriest for the sin of gluttony.

Half a fruit drops from a maple,

lost by squirrel, scolding,

who scoots to reclaim his prize.

We pause to spit a seed, juice running down our chins.

We haul our loot home in boxes, pockets,

trucks, wagons and tractors. We crave

like squirrels, and stock for winter.

Apples' last stand.

Death of a Mushroom

Just think of the noise of
the death of a mushroom:
Breath of wren
Falling snowflake
Brush of vole whiskers
Weight of fog
Passage of moth.

This is a sound that creeps
into consciousness
like a forgotten dream
felt only by the mushroom.
Reaching into the arcane world
of metaphysics, of necromancy,
philosophy of be-ing.
Which is the moment of death,
Of transformation,
Of rebirth?
The hidden mycelia
The spores
The future.

Seed to Seed

The garden spreads in May, end to end.
Broccoli, cabbage, kale, carrots, radishes, lettuce, peas and
      spinach.
Too soon for cabbage caterpillars,
the white butterfly flits by.

In June we see corn, beans and squash (the holy three),
tomatoes, beets, cucumbers, leeks, onions, peppers; and
      potatoes
over which clumsy striped beetles clamber
leaving orange eggs and fat red hungry larvae.
Stinky rough brown bugs stalk the cucumbers and squash,
leaving tarnished beads of eggs, scurrying tiny instars;
the holes, the wilt.
Biggest of all, the turgid, horrid hornworm scrapes tomato
      leaves
and fruit into ravenous mouth
leaving destruction and large brown frass.

We fight the foes and emerge victorious as seasons unravel.
Salads, lamb, venison, egg dishes grow in sophistication as
      herbs chart their fragrant progress.
Thyme, rosemary, sage and parsley (the Scarborough Fair).

Basil, bay, burnet, borage, lovage, oregano, savory, chives.
Purple buds of lavender reeling with bees of every sort.

Nevertheless, the jewel jars will fill with
emerald, ruby, amber, and topaz.
The icy vault will fill with white packages.
The shelf will bear bottles of bits of fragrant green.
Envelopes will fill with the germ of next year's bounty.

Transformation

Velociraptors rush across the barnyard

Long scaly legs

Big horny feet

Flapping wings give them away

Gobble-gobble-gobble

Thanksgiving turkeys in training

Dinosaurs for dinner

Linger

Please remember, if you may
we went into the woods today.
We saw a buck,
we heard a toad.
We lightened up our worldly load.

The trees had colored with the frost
and to the ground their leaves had tossed.
They stand erect
and unafraid
their debt to autumn goddess paid.

The bucks have rubbed on every sapling.
The orchard has succumbed to apple-ing.
The grape fern's spores
are on the breeze.
The chickadees begin to tease.

The snow geese race the coming storm.
The squirrel makes a nest that's warm,
and hides a snack
of corn and nut
to soothe the winter's gnawing gut.

The porcupine begins to waddle,

and couldn't, if he must, skedaddle.

He'll greet the spring

a sack of pins

so now he forces double chins.

The possum with his reptile tail

crawls slowly over hill and dale.

He's not as fast

as truck or car,

and crossing, doesn't get too far.

The skunk, except for awful scent,

seems somehow benevolent.

Unless he raids

the chicken coop

and spoils our plans for egg-drop soup.

The coyote makes an awful noise

when he and family sing the joys

of eating grouse,

and duck and pheasant,

which foxes also think are pleasant.

The sun goes down, the moon comes up

and soon we must go home to sup.

But yet we linger

just a bit,

and in the starlight,

quiet,

sit.

Fall Equinox

The fall equinox has inserted itself
into our lives, changing everything,
subtly and inexorably.
Our hearts are swathed in black gauze.
Our brains are weighted down
with cold gray fog.
Our eyes are infested with clouds.
When the sun does deign to shine
with harsh brilliant chill,
we shrink and cower, like vampires,
for we have perforce become creatures of the night.
The next equinox will send us outdoors,
pressing seeds into the warming earth.
We'll deal with spring's problems as best we can,
but at least infested with fewer clouds.

Butterflies of Autumn

Brown, yet not wood nymphs
yellow, not swallowtails
orange, not monarchs
arc and flutter
in the weathered woods
above the earthbound
slugs and snails

They lose altitude
regain some flight
in bits and wisps
from forest floor
until bound by damp and decay
to rise again
years hence as
saplings
decked with butterflies
till fall

Crinkles

A creeping deermouse stole

one by one

the sugarless butterscotch candies

idly left in deer blind

She cautiously nibbled the crinkly cellophane

in silence of night

before stealing away

with her prizes

sweet but empty

leaving only the crinkles

and tiny tracks

Horticide

Winter is coming. The garden's not ready.
The edges aren't mowed. The weeds are not pulled.
Grass in the candytuft, knapweed in asparagus.
Nothing is tidy, protected, or mulched.

Many plants sit in pots that should have been planted.
Trees, shrubs, and perennials, *Lilium* bulbs.
The vegetable garden, fallow all year,
is a tangle of hoses, stakes, and old weeds.

The herbs were not harvested, nor were the seeds.
The birches in pots are now growing through them.
The English oaks are still waiting so bravely,
but they cannot hang on forever for me.

The grapes have all perished, without me to tend them.
The ginkgos held on, I thank fortune for that.
The west garden leapfrogged all over, it needs work,
and the tall yucca never set seed all this year.

Farm Woodlot

Chainsaw oil

Beech sap

Beetle frass

Broken fungus

The tree sighs

cracks

and tumbles with a roar of thunder

shuddering to the soft ground

where only the pungent ramps

and seedlings of ash

survive

years of browsing by deer

hunger of Angus, Charolais

and Hereford

and their plundering hooves

Wood is pieced

with deafening precision

Silence of the deer and ghost cattle

returns

Another Year

Woodlot again.
Another year.
Another ankle-load of cockleburs.
More fuel to stoke the stove
all through the wintry blows.
Loads on the haywagon
as much as will fill the shed.

A bat flies furiously away,
her shelter gone.

See the deermouse fleeing the
hollow trunk, six babies
bouncing from her teats.

Winter again.
Another year.
Ankle-loads of ice balls
under snow pacs, snowshoeing
through the woodlot.
Heading for home and cocoa cup.
The bat's found a barn to winter in
by the woodshed.
See the tiny tracks,
weaving paths to the brushpiles we made.
Another season, another woodpile.

Planes of Days

Even as our eyes might retain
the prismatic reflections
our hearts forget
how the trees
incredulous
watch their leaves spin away
horizontal to vertical
after the long flat planes of days

Colored with crayons
they pile in restless drifts
like our thoughts
matted with snow
lie dormant till spring
when green praise emerges
like a song

The Purple Coneflower

The purple coneflower petaled
then blasted shriveled shreds
to the autumn wind
The fat prickly cones
shed seeds and bristles
from one end of the garden
to another
ensuring seedlings
too precious to be pulled as weeds
come spring

As years go along
the garden stitches itself
deeper and wider
as jumbled as memories

Old Names

Bessie, Mildred
Eliza Jane
Gertrude, Hannah
Helen CeCeal
The old names toll like bells
Echoes of schoolrooms past
Of churches and bedrooms
Of kitchens, ripe with jars
Grandmothers of grandmothers
Ancient aunts
Lost mothers and daughters

Their silent stories
Wear away
Like the limestone monuments
With names of husbands
And lost children

Abattoir

This day turned in around itself

in spirals, helices

The coiling entrails

of the sheep

The blood of the lamb

shed for me

This fractal day

This Mandelbrot set

This bloody day

Wolves

The ram lambs with their eager faces,
mouths full of fragrant hay,
are off to freezer camp.
Innocent in the falling snow,
they revel in each other's company,
companions to the end.
Their sister stands in the barn, puzzled,
reprieved for other duties.
The red trailer hauls them away.
baaing, calling,
quiet soon.

Our stomachs growl like wolves.

Snow drifts,
gently covering hoof prints.

Tupping Day

tup: a male sheep; a ram (old English)

tup: especially of a ram: copulate with

-from the Oxford English Dictionary

Fifth of November, cold day, dark skies

but blood running hot

Upheaval: rams to ewes; lambs set aside together

Bart, to Gerri and Sage- grunting, dashing, sniffing

side by side, pawing at their shoulders

Arthur to Hen and Sparrow

ignoring spits of snow and rain

This year's lambs out of sight

out of mind, next year's only imagined

Shorn flanks already wooled for winter

flank to flank, steaming

Fifth of November: Guy Fawkes's plot

to blow up Parliament

no more explosive than passions

this day, heat rising

Next generation assured when ewes stop

racing away, receptive

Ram never satisfied till December

sated, turning, lean, to sating with hay

heated water pail

fighting for dominance when

reunited, ram to ram

horns clash with forehead

Bart, bloody, loses to Arthur's big curled horns

Arthur settles in, restored.

Tupping Days, November through December

Rain to snow, heat abated

Winter:

Long Night Moon

Wolf Moon

Hunger Moon

The Harvest

Fat-bellied bags of grain
burst turgor
as mouse-nibbled corners
send spent fountains
of gold nuggets and tan
before lambs and hens
have a chance at them.
Fragrant with dust
the balance is loaded
into barrels with
mouse-proof mouths.

In the granary
cats sleep
with whiskers twitching
paws at rest.

The Crockpot

The crockpot's full of fragrant stew:

carrots, potatoes, onions

from our garden.

Rosemary and thyme

from patio pots.

Venison from our woods.

It bubbles and steams out

bursts of anticipation as

I labor outside

to fill the next pot,

and to gather eggs and berries

for the muffins.

Cedar and pine,

bluestem and goldenrod,

feed the

elusive deer.

Herb topiary,

kale and carrots,

chickens and sheep

all conspire

to fill the pot,

nourish the spirit.

No root cellar here

Our earth-sheltered home
is perforce its own root cellar
Pots of onions, red, white, and yellow
line the front hall with the boots and shoes
Pots of potatoes, red, white, and yellow
line the back hall with the coats and gloves
Bags of carrots, boxes of eggs line the fridge
Venison and lamb line the freezer
Jars of tomatoes, applesauce and sauerkraut
line the pantry shelves
No mysterious cloistered storehouse here
lined with damp earth and roots
with hidden door
We live with the fruits of our labor
as well as on them

Bark

Touch the skin of a beech:
Is it not like the elephant
with its scars of the years?
And the black cherry,
bark of blackened potato chips
flaking under your fingers
to a crinkly bag.
The maple is furrowed
like the brows of a thousand old men
contemplating the crops
And the lack of rain.
The oak, the elm, the ash,
each bearing the burden of comparison,
committing themselves to the collective mind
of the forestry class.

Six Chickens

Six chickens died today, for me
and for my family.
They spilled their blood upon the snow.
They had to go.

Those cockerels were meant since June
to meet their Doom.
They ate our oats and hay and corn.
They weren't forlorn.

They fornicated with our hens
in roomy pens.
They held contests to learn to crow
and greater grow.

The vegetable garden suffered weeks
their hungry beaks.
With cantaloupes and carrot tops
they filled their crops.

The hens went on to earn a living,
by their eggs giving.
But roosters were meant to give their meat:
a noble feat.

This may appall some city folk,
or seem a joke,
but those of us who work the Land
won't stay our hand.

We're part of Nature's greater plan,
each hungry man.
We understand the web of food
and it is good.

The fox and weasel took a few.
They're hungry too.
Our earthly lives are temporary.
We cannot tarry.

Each part of our world is connected,
intersected.
From Mother Earth we sprout and grow.
To Her we go.

Bacteria, fungi, in the end,
the compost's friend.
We live our lives and when we die
in Earth we lie.

The chickens nourish us and we
become eternity.
We live and die upon the Earth
that gave us birth.

Five

Five fringed chicken heads
lying in the snow
Bright as precious jewels
black, red and yellow.

Five bloody chicken heads
Owl thinks they're sweet
Sweeps off with her luncheon
in her taloned feet.

Four bare chicken skulls
at the garden's edge.
Weasel is happy-
it's better than vegs.

Three plucked chicken heads
now begin to stink.
One is gone quickly
found by a mink.

Two old chicken heads
waiting now to go.
Neighbor's dog is happy
Till his master says no.

One lone chicken head
chewed upon by cat.
Hauls it heavy to the grass
And that, I think is that.

Five headless chickens
plucked and gutted so,
in the freezer, safe
from weasel, dog, and snow.

Tempest in a Teapot

Steaming wee fumarole
Charms the house
Calms the cracks
Corners and chairs
Earl Grey, hot
Darjeeling with honey
Pekoe with lemon
Wonder of jasmine
Whimsy of mint
Haven of herbs
Healing and healthy

Teacakes, cookies,
Crumpets, croissants,
Butter and jam
Chocolate and cream
Grandmother's plates
Great-auntie's cups
Tempest in a teapot
At ten or at two

Winter

It's almost December.

Snow, sleet, and gale-force winds.

Bring the down down

from the attic, and mittens,

scarves, gloves, long underwear,

the mad bomber hat,

lined in rabbit.

Drink hot spiced wine,

Merlot with cinnamon and cloves.

I don't know where are the cockles of my heart,

but I know they are warm now.

Mulled wine.

Mocha cappuccino.

Comfort foods.

Comfort clothing.

Fleece and polypropylene,

wool, silk, and down.

Fat socks and bunny slippers.

Comforters and afghans.

Vivaldi and Beethoven.

Dutch cocoa, jasmine tea.

Venison stew with rosemary,

garlic, and Yukon gold potatoes.

Books of poetry, and Christmas catalogs.

Enhance the coziness by going outdoors a bit:

natural snowshoes, synthetic skis.

Write to someone

about how cold it was last night.

Revel in it:

There are no more mosquitoes.

Mice

The mice came, more and more.
Not in armies, they came in family groups;
generations visibly doubling and tripling.
Not a valise or a totebag,
they'll find everything they need within.

Cotton balls for beds.
Seeds stolen from the parrot as he sleeps
to fill new pantries, as well as catfood
and cereal, from a hole nibbled into
the back of a cardboard box, near the bottom.

They are dirty tenants,
making noise at night, and making smells.

The cat stirs on the bed,
and goes back to sleep.

Garden in Winter

Pulling leeks
leaves dry sockets
in the frozen earth.
Kale is crisp with ice,
Carrots, dug up and eaten
by the ravenous deer.
Banners of corn
flap briskly in the breeze,
their low-hanging cobs
denuded by field mice.
Onions and potatoes,
safe in bins in the house.
Ruby tomatoes in jars.
Lettuces and beans and radishes
devoured as they appeared.
Beets found by sweet-toothed rabbits.
Broccoli, steamed and stored
for cheese soup.

Garden in winter-
Echoes of gain and loss.

The Scent of Prawns

The scent of prawns
floated wispily through the rooms
in the empty house
until she returned
for a forgotten purse.
Leftover odor awoke
assaulting her senses
with last night's dinner
and its aftermath.

The Old Barn

The old barn has started to go.

The homestead, long since abandoned for the city,

and regretted, but not recovered.

A loft, stuffed with hay,

can last for longer than a house

whose windows lure stones and shot,

whose shingles are peeled by the wind,

whose basement provides creeping damp,

whose neglected faults combine to ruin.

A loft stuffed with hay,

like a sock over a darning egg,

or a shoe over a last,

retains its shape

long after the hay has lost its summer sweetness.

A fragrance not of dancing green and meadow blossom,

but of the earth, and time long past.

And if the vintage hay is hauled away,

for mulch, or to soothe a tidy whim,

or simply returns to the earthen floor,

the barn is lost.

The snows of even a winter mild

collapse the roof.

It bows like the back of a worn-out horse,

then sags and gently settles.

The winds and rains of spring complete the ruin,

and summer provides destruction in the guise of green.

Creeping, strangling vines engulf the boards.

Lichens encrust the threshold.

Field mice and wood beetles and a skunk,

replace the cows and pigs and prized horse,

of ages past.

Night Within Night

Tonight is the longest night of the year.
Drifts like white horses
pile against the ice-clear sky.
We bundle like Inuit; no sealskins,
but polartec and thinsulate.

As we forge out with the full moonlight
glistening against the frosty piles of snow,
we clutch mugs of hot chocolate,
marshmallowed against the cold.

The moon loses a splinter
slowly almost imperceptibly
and the orb wanes before our eyes
as inexorably as an old woman with a cane
working her way across the light
on her way to pluck the eggs
from under your chickens.

The moon, gone, a ghostly ember remains,
pausing in sudden transformation,
before the splinter returns
and waxes, the slice of icy pie returning
and growing into the whole.

We edge back towards

the waiting warm house.

Cinnamon toast and tea-

so early a breakfast.

Might as well stay up.

-Total Lunar Eclipse, December 21, 2010

Cornucopia

They burst forth in Midwinter,
like glorious fireworks
to celebrate the time the sun stands still
and turns around its course
to bestow upon us
the gift of the seasons of spring and summer.

Between the fold of two glossy papers
the seed catalogs burst forth
like the flashing green meteor
we saw on New Year's Eve.
A palette, a paint box.
The ninety-six box of Crayolas.

A multicolor cornucopia
of every conceivable vegetable and fruit.
Flowers in a rainbow skein
that does not miss a tint.
Wishes and hopes, sighs and dreams.
Lessons learned in the past.

We'll spend too much,
our sparkling eyes bigger than our gardens.

Trying to fit in

each new introduction, every old favorite,

choosing only to pass this year

on the turnips that went to waste last harvest.

Lessons in Country Life

The machine that harvests corn is a combine, not a combine.

The hay in the barn is in a mow, not a mow.

But you mow hay.

You can also mow with a scythe and there is still the handle

of one

in the barn under the mow.

A creek is a crick

and a face cord of wood is a rick.

If you have livestock you also have dead stock.

Bushels of oats, bales of hay.

Grandfather following grandson

as the harvest goes on.

Centennial Farm

For a time I kept my chickens
in Grandma's henhouse on the old farm.
Clucking softly, they nestled in comfort
as I collected the warm eggs.

I would go into the house,
have coffee and pie,
and learn the lore of farms
and my adopted family of in-laws.
Aunts, uncles, cousins,
grands and great-grands.
And horses, holidays,
deaths, illness, and the baby that was born
with the cord around his neck.
Stories of baptisms, dances,
celebrations of life, visits, and the first car.

And threshing dinners:
pies, pickles, potatoes, beans, rolls, chicken and hot dishes
with all the leaves in the huge table.
Wives and girls in cooking,
husbands and boys in the fields.

The uncle that was killed in an accident
with a truckload of pickles.
Selling cabbages from horse and wagon
to the Polish women in Maxwelltown.
Stories of steerage from Germany.
Smithies and lumber camps.

The harvest of pigs-
the big scalding kettle.
Witwurst, headcheese and sausage.
Lard for frying, biscuits, pies, and cakes
and spread on bread for school lunch.
Or a hot potato for school
kept in a pocket to warm hands on the long walk.

The milk cows are ghosts in the stanchions now.
The big horses Dolly and Major live only in memory.
The barn empty of the wholesome manure
that spread fields of corn,
market gardens of cabbages and corn, berries and beans.
Trial crops of peaches and shrubs.

The milkhouse remains.
The empty cooling tank for cans of cream
once held a cousin's trout.

Buried bits in the fields we find of the farm:
parts of wrenches, cultivators, apple corers;
porcelain knobs, nuts and nails,
Indian head pennies and arrowheads.

My grandchildren run now
where were the rows of beans.
The gnarled remnants of apple and pear trees
bring scant harvest of sweet fruit.
Rusted horse-drawn rakes and plows,
scythes and corn-knives
remain as reminders
of hard work, hardships and joy.

Crop Damage Permits

In the winters of the late '80s
marauding deer (de-)ranged
across the countryside
behind their mouths
Consuming crops
With consummate success
Corn, winter wheat
Shearing our fields of shrubs
ravaged by the row
Thuja, Taxus, Euonymus

Deer, shot in the snow
filled many a freezer
Few were left downed
in the fields with their friends
Twin fetuses in a jar of
formaldehyde graced the school lab

Across the county
by thousands they came
behind their mouths
Doubling, tripling the legions of coyotes
whose mouths then decimate the deer

following the fawns as they fell

behind their mothers

Growing, and growing silent

As many as the stones

Returning to the stones

from whence they came

Soup

Pawing herbs from snowy crust,

pulling leeks from frozen earth,

cutting crisp kale, spared by cottontails.

Potatoes binned in baskets in the laundry room.

Simmer all in broth of fall-killed hens.

Sage and thyme haunt the house,

an afternoon drowse with book and tea.

(Ignore the roiling cauldron at your peril.)

Garden returns to winter rest,

sleeping under snow,

spring not yet a dream.

Weekly Shopping

in the same familiar store.
I know the way.
I grasp the lettuces, to choose
the best, the firmest;
no discoloration.
It all matters so much.
The carrots lie parallel in their plastic.
Choose the most uniform.
The most perfect.
Alas, I won't be taking celery home today.
Just look at it.

The oranges in their mesh bags
celestial orbs, all the same
and yet different... each
with a certain asymmetry of form.
Choose at last.
I shall use the lacy bag for fat
for the woodpeckers, the chickadees,
the titmice, and oh, dear,
the bluejays.

And here I am at last.
Must I ask the butcher for the suet,

and disturb his *sanctum sanctorum*,
"Authorized Personnel Only"?

The dry goods, the boxes and cans and bags
line up carefully. If I take one,
the order is disturbed.
Shall I move one over to fill the gaping space
or would that lead to so much more?
I dare not go there. I take the can of cranberries anyway
leaving a socket like a missing tooth.

The cart fills slowly.
The decisions are exhausting.
It all matters
so very much.

the sound of snow

the sound of claws, feathering across the drifts
beaking up sunflower seeds
leaving trails of husks and chaff

the sound of snow from the west
crispy bits, duck down, edged in tatted lace
matrix for wings, feathering through the flakes

the sound of paws, rappelling oak trees
scattering tight-fisted acorns
that plop to the drift, disappearing with no trace

the sound of long skis slicing, speeding
squeaking, buried in froth, swishing like a breeze
the thunk of poles, hot breath, the drip of red nose

the sound of moths inside the window
mirroring the vision outside, fluffy with soft scales
wearying of the cold, falling

the sound of mini-marshmallows in cocoa
releasing tiny bubbles of sweet air
the tonguing up, the slurp, the sigh

133

the sound of airy comforter

soaring and settling over bed

snuggling warmth and weariness

Moons of Year's End

Harvest Moon

Summer wanes.
Pullet eggs finally appear.
Tomatoes finish,
reds already in jars,
greens abandoned
to the frost.

Hunter's Moon

Autumn waxes.
Leaves burgeon into flame
and drop
as spent
as the deer's violent end.
Pumpkins are harvested,
become faces
that sink to mush.
Geese vee overhead
with their strident farewell.

Frost Moon

Wet black branches lash
against lasting gales.
Ships founder and are lost.
More deer fall until
turkey's met with relief and regret.
Nights barely fade into days

Long Night Moon

Mood sinks to winter rains
and sleet.
Sodden
under drifts and
thaws, rotten ice
followed again and again
by fresh flakes
that sink under their own weight.
Year's end.

As Winter Stalked

across the whirling countryside,

pale moon could not pierce clouds.

Brown eggs froze under hens in the barn.

Snow piled high on the warm wooly sheep

as they waited in the field.

Cats whiskered, turned, and curled up in the hay.

Fingernails grew brittle and cracked,

and our dry skin itched under heavy clothes.

We put rolled towels against doorsills' draft.

The stove took logs of birch and beech

with the hunger of a prowling wolf,

before we sought comfort of quilts.

Fawns faltered in tall drifts as

coyotes waited, awake.

Voles slept unaware

under meadow grass.

Not a creature stirred

this twenty-fourth night

of December.

Season

Snow slips from the slickery sky
whirling in wispy cyclones
over covered grass.
The lawn won't be mown all winter.

Skeleton trees lace the air,
whirling reds and yellows
supplanted by whirling white.
Red shovels replace rakes.

Whirling my thoughts
spring forward, summer satisfaction
falls back as do winter melancholy and
ennui. Go forth, with

slippery skis, slick sleds
and duckfooted snowshoes.
Take crisp air inside
dormant bodies. Break forth!

Do not slide into sadness
whose tentacles embrace even
snowflakes. The birds flick around.
Why can't we?

After somber stillness of inches,

flakes fly up and twinkle,

luring us, mufflers and mittens,

to sunshine or to starlight to play.

Year of the Possum

The New Year is an opossum.

This is not

my favorite animal.

They eat eggs and chicks and catfood.

They hide under the hay

where they are safe

from my guns,

my crowbars,

my bare hands, I swear.

They grin, always,

an evil, mocking grimace.

A death (that word that means rigor mortis):

you can't tell if they are dead or alive.

They can be alive if they are dead

playing possum.

Our old dog used to bring them home, proud,

and bury them to season the meat.

When he lay down,

possum would get up and move off,

not too fast, not too slow,

just kind of a relentless progress,

cold blooded, reptilian,

an aura enhanced by the furless tail.

The New Year is not a phoenix
rising from the ashes of the Old Year.
It is not a diapered caricature of a baby,
dewy with promise,
vanquisher of the Old Year,
grey, stooped Grim Reaper
with his scythe dulled
by 365 days of hard use.
The New Year is not a wagging puppy,
destined for companionable maturity.
It is not a glorious dragon.
It is an opossum.

It creeps out by night
thriving on the offal of civilization.
They are born fetuses
So they begin life
as an abortion.

They bring no Hope,
only the Certainty
that no matter how many are killed by cars,
refusing to rot by the side of the road,
more will appear, and more,
as inexorable as the March of Years.

Another possum,
another year.
Dead or alive,
as infinite and fixed
as the stars.

September Dewberries in January

Turgid droplets of ebony juice
Delicate as the thought of a thunderstorm
Promise of pleasure
Redolent of raspberries
After the pain of plucking
precious fruit from reluctant canes
treasure can burst upon the tongue
snatching glory from flaky crust
Or, discipline the mouth
for the postponed joy of jam
Fruit picked over, washed of
tarnished diamond bugs, green aphids
leaves, snagged clouds, bits of breeze
Measured into a kettle
Snowdrifts of sugar
Boiling and bubbling
toiling and troubling
until bounty is ladled into jars
covered with wax
tidy as bees' cells of honey
Glowing with the radioactive fervor
of pent-up suns on pantry shelves

Today, drifts of sugar

cover the barren brambles

Gone the bees

Gone the sun

Gone the sweaty bloody sacrifice

Today, taste of late summer

comes to glorious life

Tumbling over a waffle,

wheat toast, a scone

Bruised lips

Thunderstorm on the tongue

Seeds stuck fast in teeth

Scent of blossoms

Sweet joy in long-patient mouth

Patience rewarded

Tributes of toil

in the blessings of the bloom

Kitchen Hiatus

The tapioca denatured into glorious vanilla

soup as it simmered

overlong on the stove the flame

the froth the failure

we ate it gratefully

the bread rose overlong was

punched in again and

rose to giddy heights

but alas left the oven too soon

as an indecent antidote to

the pudding

we ate it gratefully

at least the kitchen throbbed with life

again

Fire

Scratch pen across paper

as if to strike a match

Strike-anywhere not

Strike-on-box

Not always a box

to strike

Strike on zipper fly

hearth, rock

or if you can

your fingernail poof!

A tiny flame

Touch it to paper or a tiny teepee

with birchbark strips whoosh!

A warming or cleansing fire

Gone is the cold or the trash

in a sudden glow like distant suns

with unknown balls of

rock and gas for company

Flowers in the furnace

Circle of rocks

Ashes ashes we all fall down

Posies on the end of tiny sulfur stick

Strike anywhere

Fire

The Silence Echoed

between the huge downy flakes

of lake effect snow

this January day

this ice-fresh new year.

Flutter of chickadees

absorbed by whiteness

made no sound as audible

as the snow.

Luminous, it piled inches and inches

upon the branches of the weeping mulberry,

the towering Norway spruce,

the ebony arms of the skeletal maple.

Eyelashes,

feathers,

thoughts,

and high above the clouds,

on the arms of the crescent moon.

Treasure

We found an antler last year
tucked shy among dewberry vines
near the field where morels grow
and the old orchard that poison ivy found

Voles and porcupines had
gnawed off the points
weathered toothmarks still showing
on the graying surface

No bones nearby, it was
shed fair and square in early
winter, no part of lost
wounded prize or mishap
on gravel road

We carried it home to nestle it
with cushions of reindeer moss,
Petoskey stones, bird nests,
groundstars and other treasures

on the mantle, over hearth lit
with burning twigs shaped like

antlers, stones, and nests

of seasons past

and seasons yet to come

Wiggle and Twist

The cat watches the gerbils
from a pile of books.
They wiggle and twist
in a bed of paper curls.
They whisker from me
carrots and crackers,
cherries and cheese.

The cat sighs
closes her eyes
and dreams
of wiggle and twist.

little snowflakes

the clock ticking off the hours and days since the plow has

gone by

slows perceptibly

little snowflakes build into drifts against the house

and barn doors

tick

tick

tick

we go out to shovel again, and again, piling into tunnels

around walks and drives

and return to cozy house for tea and toast

the road disappears as we watch for hours

for the plodding plow to go by

it doesn't

we knead bread and watch it rise

in our new continuum as time slows again

the bread bakes, we slice and toast

and prepare the cinnamon sugar with growing anticipation

as the snowflakes pile up once and once again

the amber tea steeps slowly into the clear boiled water

Tastes of Late Winter

the biscuits were light as a feather
the pound cake was rich, deep and moist
lamb stew was outstanding
the chili, so frisky
enlivening the dark winter days

pie made with wizening apples
rings made with onions that sprout
use wrinkled late storage potatoes
for soup, for escalloped, for mashed

cook your way through until it is springtime
stew through the long winter nights
bake cookies, dark brownies and wheat bread
and work it all off in deep snow

with spring come fresh snowpeas and spinach
kale sprung from the snowbanks, from fall
brook trout, red strawberries and lettuce
the seasons come through after all

Shrugging Winter From My Shoulders
(Fukushima 2011)

Crunching the layer of ice over puddles

I walk into a March morning where

doves proclaim their mournful love

Cardinals whistle

Cranes clatter across the back field

Deer emerge in daylight, seeking green to graze

on widening spaces in drifted fields

Lace overlays footprints in crusty snow

Rabbits scavenge seeds

revealed under feeders

The moon is at perigee

A world away

the rabbit on the moon

pounds rice for rice cakes

Snow sifts to the ground

Reactor fires flame clouds

over devastated towns as

quakes continue over a trashed scape

Bodies wash up on beaches

Yet the plum trees will blossom

as days lengthen in our shared latitudes

under the same moon

Echoes

The echoes I hear on this farm are not my echoes
They are the echoes of a farm that fed a family and a nation
through the Great Depression and two world wars
with hoe and chicken
hog and garden
field and orchard
My husband's grandpa
and his father before
milked cows in those dusty stanchions
walked crops behind big horses
Dolly and Major
who dragged the stones out of the fields
on stone boats
hauled the wood that fed the stove
that fed the threshers
who threshed the grain
that the grain binder fed
plowed, harrowed and planted
corn that was picked
husked and shelled
Hay was mowed, raked, and forked
onto huge wagon loads
before being carefully stacked in the mow
by hard-won skill

Grandpa's family were Germans from

Soltnitz, now in Poland

From farms

and from blacksmithing

a craft that was drafted into

following Teutonic war horses

to battle after battle, until

they left for America in steerage

leaving five children behind

in the ground in Prussia

The S.S. Main from Bremen to Baltimore

with all their children and a featherbed

to work at the lumber mills in Filer City

until they farmed again

Grandma's family came from Germany

to a prosperous farm in Indiana

(Why did they leave it?)

to the farm in Michigan

She swore she'd never marry a farmer

But Herman cut a rug

in dances, and the Lutheran church was

down the road between their two farms

He stole her heart in a cutter

over snowy drifts

They spent fifty-five years together
with five children (one lost at birth,
a tangled cord)
On to thirteen grandchildren
with thirteen appliqued quilts
crafted in tiny proud stitches
on the quilt frame in the gray house
beneath the maples
the show-stopping rhododendron
the champion Norway spruce
Grandma told of how she preferred
work outdoors rather
than housework, though she'd
cook, and clean, and can, and quilt
with the best of them
She sewed tiny flannel shirts for my sons
her great-grands

She taught me how to garden
to can those quarts of fruits and vegetables
jam and sauerkraut and pickles
how to raise chicks and hens and gather the eggs
roosters for meat
how to kill, scald, pluck, singe and dress
until I could do it in no time flat
how to pitch in when the hay must

race the coming storm to the big red barn

how to host the family dinners, four generations

with three kinds of pie and homemade rolls

This farm, this family has become my own

Heart and history

Love and tears

In sickness and in health

Till we can farm no more.

Made in the USA
Middletown, DE
19 April 2015